# Christi

Preheat oven to 4

Mix these ingredients thoroughly:
1/2 cup sugar
1 cup margarine
1 egg
3 tsp vanilla or almond flavoring

Add:
3 cups flour
1/2 tsp. baking powder

Use a cookie press to make some
of your favorite shapes.

Bake 5-7 min.

Makes 5-6 dozen cookies.

## GiGi's Gingersnaps

3/4 cup butter softened
1 cup dark brown sugar, firmly packed
1 egg
1/4 cup molasses
2 cup flour
1/4 tsp. salt
2 tsp. baking soda
1 tsp. ginger
1 tsp. cinnamon
1 tsp. ground cloves

Combine butter, sugar and egg in mixing bowl, beat until fluffy. Add molasses, beat well. Add dry ingredients, mix well. Chill dough. Shape into 1" balls and roll in sugar. Bake at 350° for 12-15 minutes on a greased baking sheet or parchment paper. Makes 4 dozen cookies.

—Eula

# CHRISTMAS at HOME

### Quilts for Your Holiday Traditions

By Christina DeArmond,
Eula Lang and
Kaye Spitzli

# CHRISTMAS at HOME
## Quilts for Your Holiday Traditions

By Christina DeArmond, Eula Lang and Kaye Spitzli

Editor: Deb Rowden
Designer: Bob Deck
Photography: Aaron T. Leimkuehler
Illustration: Lon Eric Craven
Technical Editor: Deb McCurnin
Production assistance: Jo Ann Groves

Published by:
Kansas City Star Books
1729 Grand Blvd.
Kansas City, Missouri, USA 64108

First edition, second printing
ISBN: 978-1-935362-09-8

Library of Congress Control Number:
2009923429

Printed in the United States of America by
Walsworth Publishing Co., Marceline, MO

To order copies, call StarInfo at (816) 234-4636
and say "Books."

KANSAS CITY STAR
QUILTS
Continuing the Tradition

PickleDish.com
The Quilter's Home Page

# Dedication

We dedicate this book to our grandchildren. Christina's cuties; Will and Brady. Eula's darlings; Zion, Jonah, Sophia, Evangeline, Eliana, Solveigh, and Lotus (a new grandchild!). Kaye's sweethearts; Lakin, Paige, Joe, Mindy and Mike. You inspire us to pass on our Christmas traditions, may you find joy in them and continue to pass the heritage on to your own families in years to come.

Love,
*Grandma Christy*
*Grandma Eula*
*Nana Kaye*

# Acknowledgements

We are so appreciative of you great quilters who purchase our books. We enjoy sharing our designs with you and hope these will enhance your own Christmas celebrations for years to come!

Our mothers are always ready to help out: Elizabeth Slankard, Arlene Lawson, and our honorary mom Pat Black helped with embroidery and piecing. Thank you for your help and support.

Thank you to the world's best quilt photographer, Aaron Leimkuehler. Your eye for detail and creativity always amazes us—thank you!

Deb Rowden: thank you for your great gift of organization which you put into practice in managing our work. Your gentle reminders and friendly urging keep us moving forward on schedule as well.

Our beautiful book design is due to the talents of Bob Deck. Your creativity is so appreciated, thank you for the beautiful work.

Thank you to the great Kansas City Star Books crew—Doug Weaver, Diane McClendon, Jo Ann Groves, Lon Eric Craven, and Deb McCurnin—who each do their part in making beautiful quilt books a reality.

# Contents

Introduction    6
About the Authors    7

## Projects

Christmases Remembered Quilt    10
Behold That Star Quilt    16
     Twilling Instructions    21
Deck the Halls Table Runner    22
I'll Be Home for Christmas
     Table Runner or Tree Skirt    26
O Tannenbaum Quilt    30

# Introduction

Christmas memories hold a treasured spot in the heart. This book will aid you in making quilted Christmas memories for your family.

The first two quilts, **Christmases Remembered** and **Behold That Star**, combine pieced star blocks with 20 embroidered blocks.

Two smaller projects also draw from those patterns. **I'll be Home for Christmas** uses your choice of four of the embroidered blocks with easy, but striking, piecing to make a lovely tree skirt or tabletopper. **Deck the Halls** uses the same pieced star to make an innovatively shaped coordinating table runner.

**O Tannenbaum** is a beautiful Christmas Tree wallhanging. It's a fun addition to your Christmas décor or a "no watering required" alternative to a real tree—the perfect quilt for anyone without space for a large tree.

Enjoy this book and make Happy Christmas memories for your loved ones!

*Christy, Eula and Kaye*

# About the Authors

## Eula Lang

Christmas is all about remembering and giving. I think of the birth of Jesus Christ, Himself a gift from Father God. The gift He gave of Himself as a sacrifice gives this day its meaning for me. All my life, I have gathered with loved ones at this time of the year to remember and celebrate. As the years go by, there are more memories and more people to share those memories with.

In my childhood, our celebrations centered around family: my parents, four brothers, and two sisters. There was always a tree and stockings, but my strongest memories are of the warm feelings of togetherness and the tastes of those Christmas goodies—Mom's fudge, divinity and cinnamon rolls. I remember waking Dad and Mom at the crack of dawn and tumbling down the stairs on Christmas morning to see the tree surrounded by gifts.

When I met and married my husband, Rob, I was introduced to his family's traditions which included his Grandma Arnesen's (GiGi's) gingersnap cookies. These became a staple in our family traditions as our four children, Breezy, Luke, Caleb and Zach, arrived and grew up. As our children grew and became nosey package shakers, I started the tradition of wrapping their gifts in odd packages (canisters, bowls) and making a new secret code each year. Instead of putting names on gifts, they would be marked with a code that wasn't revealed until Christmas morning!

These days, our family has expanded with the addition of three wonderful daughter-in-laws—Jenny, Morgan and Molly—and six (soon to be seven) delightful grandchildren. We blend our old traditions with the new, as we wake up in the morning to open gifts, share the traditional goodies, and the love and warmth of family.

May all your Christmas memories be warm and happy ones!

## Christina DeArmond

Christmas has always been my very favorite time of year. As a child, I remember being so excited that Santa Claus was going to come that I would go to bed extremely early so he could arrive earlier. I shared a bedroom with two sisters. We would lay awake and try not to talk so we could fall asleep. Of course, it always took hours to finally fall asleep.

My other memories revolve around family. My family is very important to me and Christmas would not be the same if I didn't have them to share it with. I am one of five children and we are very close. All five of us have married, had children and now grandchildren. Our extended family now numbers 42 and we still have a great time getting together as often as possible, although space is starting to become a problem. Christmas memories always bring warmth to my heart: reading Christmas cards, playing games, drinking hot chocolate while decorating the tree, and of course, Christmas carols. I hope that as you make these quilts and other projects, many wonderful Christmas memories will warm your heart.

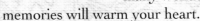

# Kaye Spitzli

As a child living in a small town with family all around, Christmas was always celebrated with church, children's programs, and family dinners.

One strong memory from my childhood took place at my Grandparents' house. Mom and Dad had the wood floors refinished at our house and we weren't able to move back home until after the holiday. Grandma's house was heated with a coal stove in the basement and open registers allowed heat to flow up through the house. That was the year my brother got his electric train set. He and I woke up in the night hearing the train and peeked down through the register to see "Santa's helpers" enjoying the new train in the dining room below!

When John and I married, we had no ornaments. We trimmed our first tree with knitted booties, bells and tiny boxes made from a cracker box. Each year since, we have included ornaments from the previous years while adding a new handmade ornament. My father is a wood carver and we have several of his original ornaments on our tree.

In the 1980s, we spent a few years in South America and our tree includes many ornaments made there. Our first Christmas outside the US was in Costa Rica. There we strung popcorn and hung tiny candy canes on our "Charlie Brown" tree…this was definitely a learning experience as ants carried away our tree days before Christmas arrived! When we were in Colombia, we had a "tropical" tree made by wrapping a tree branch with cotton. This took hours, but produced a beautiful tree.

Now that I am a grandma, our Christmas traditions involve the grandchildren. We enjoy baking cookies together, then decorating the tree, and they also like to help me set out my nativity collection.

## Aunt Sharon's Sugar Cookies

The sour cream is the key ingredient of this recipe to provide soft sugar cookies. They will get crispy, but not rock hard if stored in a sealed container.

4 cups flour
1 cup butter
2 eggs
1 1/2 cup sugar
1/2 cup sour cream
1 tsp. baking soda
1/2 tsp. vanilla

Mix flour and butter together, set aside. Beat eggs until fluffy. Add sugar, sour cream and flavoring. Mix with flour mixture and chill overnight.

Roll out on lightly floured area and cut with cookie cutter shapes. Bake at 350° for 7-9 minutes. Makes about 3 dozen average size cookies.

## Frosting for Sugar Cookies

2 cups powdered sugar
1/2 cup butter
1/2 tsp. cream of tartar
dash of salt
1/2 tsp. almond flavoring

Mix together, after thorough blending, add one unbeaten egg white and mix..

Spread on the cookies and add sprinkles.

Enjoy.

Projects

# Christmases Remembered
## 93" x 105"

Stitched by Christina DeArmond and Pat Black, embroidered by Elizabeth Slankard, quilted by Eula Lang

Christmastime holds vivid memories for all of us. As a child, I remember getting up early on Christmas morning. I waited anxiously at the top of the stairs for Dad to go down and turn on the Christmas lights so all seven of us kids could pour down the steps and see all the presents that had magically multiplied overnight! My childhood Christmas memories also include a basket Mom filled with the Christmas cards as they arrived. I would look through the cards at the beautiful pictures and read the messages from family and friends, many who lived far away.

When designing this quilt, we used the inspiration of those cards for the embroidered blocks. I hope that this quilt will evoke cozy, happy Christmas memories for you as well.

*Eula*

*"Behold, I bring you good news of great joy which will be for all the people; for today in the city of David there has been born for you a Savior, who is Christ the Lord."*

Luke 2:10b-11

### Abbreviations

These abbreviations are used throughout the quilt instructions:

**hst** = half-square triangle (a square cut in half diagonally once)

**qst** = quarter-square triangle (a square cut in half diagonally twice)

**wof** = width of fabric

## Fabric Requirements

- Cream—2 ¼ yards background for the embroidery blocks
- White or cream fabric or interfacing—2 ¼ yards for lining (if needed)
- Cream print-large scale—⅓ yard for the star centers
- Gold—1 yard for the star points
- Green floral print—1 ½ yards for the star background
- Red tonal—1 ⅔ yards for the star centers and setting triangles
- Dark green—¾ yard for the inner border
- Red print—⅔ yard for the hourglass border
- Green print—⅔ yard for the hourglass border
- Cream print—1 yard (small scale) for the hourglass border
- Brown print—1 ¼ yards for border 3 and binding
- Large print—2 ¾ yards for the outer border
- Pigma or jelly roll pens
- Embroidery thread

## Cutting Directions

**From the cream background cut:**
- 20 - 11" squares

**From the large scale cream print cut:**
- 30 - 3 ½" squares

**From the gold cut:**
- 60 - 4 ¼" squares, cut in half diagonally twice to make a total of 240 quarter-square triangles (qst)

**From the green floral cut:**
- 120 - 3 ½" squares for the star block corner squares
- 30 - 4 ¼" squares, cut in half diagonally twice to make a total of 120 qst

**From the red tonal cut:**
- 5 - 14" squares, cut in half diagonally twice to make 20 qst. Only 18 are needed for the top, bottom, and side setting triangles
- 2 - 7 ¼" squares cut in half diagonally once to make a total of 4 half-square triangles (hst). These are the corner setting triangles.
- 30 - 4 ¼" squares cut in half diagonally twice to make a total of 120 qst

11

## Borders

***Note:*** *The top, bottom and side borders are different sizes to make the hourglass border fit correctly.*

**From the dark green for the inner border cut:**
**For the sides:**
- 4 strips 2 ³/₈" x width of fabric (wof).

**For the top and bottom:**
- 4 strips 2 ³/₄" strips x wof.

**Hourglass border:**
**From the red print for the hourglass border cut:**
- 18 - 5 ³/₄" squares, cut in half diagonally twice to make 72 qst. You need 70.

**From the green print for the hourglass border cut:**
- 18 - 5 ³/₄" squares, cut in half diagonally twice to make 72 qst. You need 70.

**From the small scale cream print for the hourglass border cut:**
- 36 - 5 ³/₄" squares, cut in half diagonally twice to make 144 qst. You need 140.

**From the brown print cut:**
- 9 - 2" strips x wof for border 3
- 10 - 2 ¹/₂" x wof strips for binding

**From the large print for the outer border cut**
*lengthwise:*
- Two 6 ¹/₂" x 93 ¹/₂" strips for side borders
- Two 6 ¹/₂" x 92" strips for the top and bottom borders

## Piecing Instructions

### Embroidery Blocks

Using a light box, carefully center each picture **on point** onto one of the 11" squares of cream background fabric. Trace the pattern lines using a Pigma or Jelly Roll pen. Choose an ink color that matches the embroidery floss. If desired, embroidery squares may be lined with a plain fabric or interfacing to prevent thread tails from showing through on the right side of fabric.

Lay the block fabric over the floss: if the floss is visible through the fabric, line the blocks. Baste or fuse the lining or interfacing to the blocks before beginning the stitching. Embroider the designs using the stem stitch. When completed press the blocks from the back side. Trim each block to 9 ¹/₂", taking care to keep the design centered.

### Star Blocks

**1.** Pair 120, 4 ¹/₄" gold qst with 120, 4 ¹/₄" red qst right sides together. Stitch along the short side to form 120 gold/red triangles (unit 1). Do not reverse the color order – sew these as shown below.

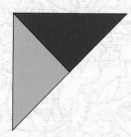

**2.** Repeat using the remaining 120, 4 ¹/₄" gold qst and 120 green floral 4 ¹/₄" qst. Stitch along the short side to form 120 gold/green floral triangles (unit 2). Do not reverse the color order – sew these as shown below.

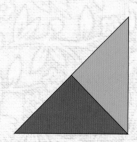

**3.** Sew unit 1 to unit 2. Repeat with the remaining 119 sets for a total of 120 sets of 3 ½" Hourglass units which are red/gold – green/gold.

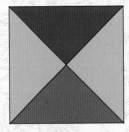

**4.** Assemble the rows. Row 1: 3 ½" green floral square, hourglass unit, 3 ½" green floral square.

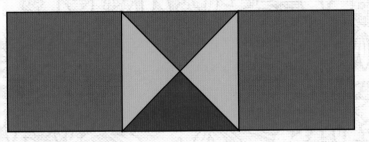

**5.** Row 2: hourglass unit, 3 ½" large scale cream print, hourglass unit.

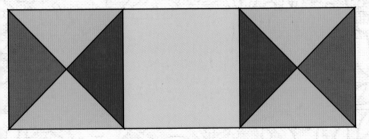

**6.** Row 3: 3 1/2" green floral square, hourglass unit, 3 1/2" green floral square.

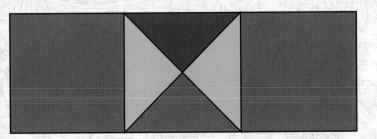

**7.** Sew the rows together to complete the star blocks.

## Assembling the Quilt

**1.** Sew together the embroidery blocks, the star blocks and the red side setting triangles and corner setting triangles into diagonal rows as shown.

**2.** Sew the rows together.

## Dark Green Inner Border

**1.** Sew together the 4 - 2 ⅜" x wof dark green strips. Cut 2 - 2 ⅜" x 77" strips. Sew 1 strip to each side of the quilt.

**2.** Sew together the 4 - 2 ¾" x wof dark green strips. Cut 2 - 2 ¾" x 68" strips. Sew a strip to the top and to the bottom of the quilt.

## Hourglass Border

**1.** Following the same method used to make hourglass units in the star blocks, pair the 70 - 5 ¾" green print qst with 70 of the 5 ¾" cream print qst, and stitch together along the short side. Pair 70 - 5 ¾" red print qst with the remaining 70 - 5 ¾" cream print qst, and stitch together along the short side.

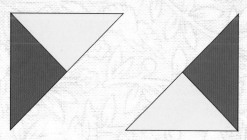

**2.** Pair each cream/green unit with a red/cream unit, right sides together with the 2 cream print triangles on opposite sides.

**3.** Stitch together to form 70 hourglass blocks (measuring 5", to finish at 4 ½").

**4.** Sew 2 strips of 18 hourglass blocks together. Sew 1 strip to each side of the quilt.

**5.** Sew 2 strips of 17 blocks together. Sew 1 strip to the top and one to the bottom of the quilt.

## Brown Print Border

**1.** Sew 5 brown print 2" x wof strips together, then cut 2 - 2" x 90 ½" strips. Sew 1 to each side of the quilt.

**2.** Sew 4 brown print 2" x wof strips together, then cut 2 - 2" x 80" strips. Sew a strip to the top and to the bottom of the quilt.

## Outer Large Print Border

**1.** Sew a 6 ½" x 93 ½" large print strip to each side of the quilt.

**2.** Sew a 6 ½" x 92" large print strip to the top and the bottom of the quilt.

## Finishing

Quilt as desired. Sew together the 10 - 2 ½" brown print strips and bind.

**Assembly Diagram**

# Behold That Star

## 57" x 70"

Stitched by Christina DeArmond, quilted by Eula Lang

It's time to come home. Do you remember the Christmas stories of loved ones who are away from their families during the holidays and need to make their way home? When they finally get close, they see candles lit in the windows to welcome them home. That's what Christmas is to me. It is those warm, fuzzy feelings that spread the warm glow that make Christmas so special.

*Christina*

"Let your light so shine before men, that they may see your good works, and glorify your Father which is in heaven."

Matt. 5:16

## Materials Needed

- 6 skeins of DMC size 5 perle cotton color #783 or embroidery floss of your choice
- Size 7 crewel embroidery needle
- Pigma pen
- Cream background fabric for twilling or embroidery—1 yard
- Muslin to be used for lining twilled blocks —1 yard
- Dark gold fabric for stars (a mixture of 2-4 dark gold prints)—a total of 2 yards
- Light gold fabric for stars (a mixture of 2-4 light gold prints)—a total of 1 ½ yards
- Dark gold/ brown fabric for inner border —⅓ yard
- Gold fabric for side setting triangles, outer border and binding—3 yards

## Cutting Directions

### From the cream background cut:
- 12 - 10 ½" squares

### From the dark gold for stars cut:
- 80 - 3 ½" squares – cut these in sets of 4 so that the corner squares in each star match.
- 20 - 4 ¼"squares, cut in half diagonally twice to make 80 quarter square triangles (qst): these will be the outer triangles in the star blocks.

### From the light gold fabrics for stars cut:
- 20 - 3 ½" squares for the star centers
- 60 - 4 ¼" squares, cut in half diagonally twice to make 240 qst—cut 20 sets of 2 squares to make the star points match within each star. The remaining 20 squares are used 1 per star, mix and match them as desired.

### From dark gold/brown for the inner border cut:
- 6 - 1 ¼" strips

### From the gold for setting triangles cut:
- 4 - 14" squares cut in half diagonally twice to make 16 qst. Only 14 of these qst will be used for the top, bottom and side setting triangles.
- 2 - 7 ¼" squares cut in half diagonally once to make a total 4 our half square triangles (hst) for the corner setting triangles

### Outer border and binding cut lengthwise:
- 4 strips 5" x 74" for outer borders
- 4 strips 2 ½" x 74" for binding

## Piecing Instructions

### Twilling or Embroidery Blocks
Carefully center then trace each picture **on point** on one of the 10 1/2" pieces of cream background fabric using a Pigma, or Jelly Roll pen. Choose a color that matches the embroidery floss. You may line these blocks if necessary as directed on page 12. Twill the designs according to the instructions on page 21 or embroider the designs using the stem stitch. When twilling or embroidery is completed, press the blocks then trim them to 9 1/2", being careful to keep the design centered.

# Star Blocks

**1.** For each block pair 4 light gold, 4 ¼" qst with 4 - 4 ¼"dark gold qst right sides together. Stitch along the short side to form 4 light gold/dark gold triangles (unit 1).

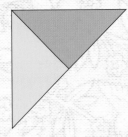

**2.** Repeat, using 4 light gold 4 ¼" qst that match those in unit 1 and 4 dark gold 4 ¼" qst that are a different fabric from those in unit 1. Stitch along the short side to form 4 light gold/dark gold triangles (unit 2).

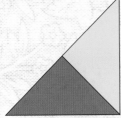

**3.** Sew unit 1 to unit 2. You now have 4 matching hourglass units.

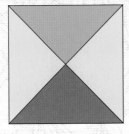

**4.** Using 4- 3 ½" dark gold squares that match the dark gold in the hourglass blocks and a coordinating or matching light gold square assemble the star as shown:

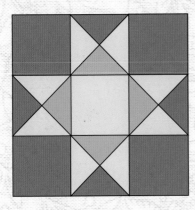

**5.** Repeat to make a total of 20 blocks. Blocks will measure 9 ½".

## Assembling the Blocks

**1.** Sew together the twilled/embroidery blocks, the star blocks and the gold side setting triangles and corner setting triangles into diagonal rows as shown below.

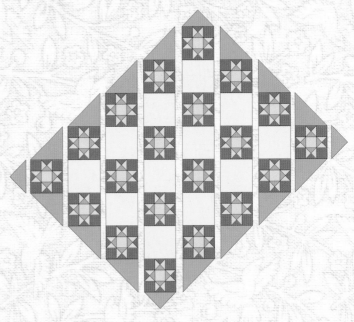

**2.** Sew the rows together.

**3.** Sew the dark gold/brown inner border strips together and cut 2 - 64 ⅛" strips. Sew 1 to each side of the quilt.

**4.** Cut 2 - 52 ¹⁵⁄₁₆" strips, sew 1 to each the top and the bottom of the quilt.

**5.** Sew a gold outer border strip to each of the 4 sides of the quilt. Center the strips on each side and miter the corners.

## Finishing

Quilt as desired. Sew the gold binding strips together and attach to the quilt.

*Enjoy your golden memories!*

**Assembly Diagram**

# Twilling Instructions

**3.** With the thread on the left side, pass the needle under the previous stitch from right to left without going through the fabric. Pull gently.

**4.** With the thread on the left side, pass the needle again under the same stitch from right to left without going through the fabric. Pull gently to make a nice knot.

**5.** Repeat these steps to complete the design.

**1.** Bring needle up from the back.

**2.** With the thread on the top side, make a small stitch from right to left approx. 1/8" from where the thread came up. Be careful not to pull the stitch too tightly.

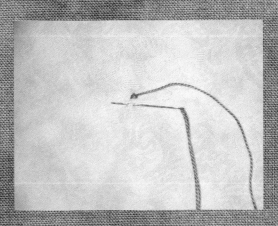

# Deck the Halls Tablerunner
## 40" x 26"

Stitched by Christina DeArmond, quilted by Eula Lang

# Fabric Requirements

- Light gold background—½ yard
- Dark gold star points—¼ yard
- Medium-gold triangles around the star center—¼ yard
- Darkest gold star centers—⅛ yard
- Deep gold or light brown—⅓ yard

The yardage listed above is for five fabrics only: I used more fabrics for a controlled scrappy look. To achieve this look, vary the fabrics from star to star, but use just one background fabric, one star point fabric and one fabric for the triangles around the Star center per block.

*"Sing we joyous, all together*
*Fa la la, la la la, la la la*
*Heedless of the wind and weather...."*
— Deck the Halls

# Cutting Directions

**From the light gold background cut:**
- 28 - 3 ½" squares
- 7 - 4 ¼" squares, cut in half diagonally twice to make 28 quarter-square triangles (qst)

**From the dark gold for star points cut:**
- 14 - 4 ¼" squares, cut in half diagonally twice to make 56 qst

**From the medium-gold triangles around the star center cut:**
- 7 - 4 ¼" squares, cut in half diagonally twice to make 28 qst

**From the darkest gold star centers cut:**
- 7 - 3 ½" squares

**From deep gold or light brown cut:**
- 2 - 1" x width of fabric (wof) strips- cut into 8 - 1" x 9 ½" strips for sashing
- 2 - 1" squares for cornerstones
- 3 - 2 ½" x wof strips for binding

# Piecing Instructions

## Star Blocks

1. For *each block* pair 4 light gold, 4 ¼" qst with 4 - 4 ¼" dark gold qst, right sides together. Stitch along the short side to form 4 dark gold/ light gold triangles (unit 1).

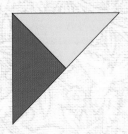

2. Repeat, using 4 dark gold 4 ¼" qst and 4 medium-gold 4 ¼" qst. Stitch along the short side. You now have 4 dark gold/medium-gold triangles (unit 2).

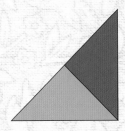

3. Sew unit 1 to unit 2. Repeat until you have 4 matching hourglass units which measure 3 ½".

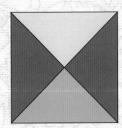

4. Assemble rows. Row 1: 3 ½" light gold square, hourglass unit, 3 ½" light gold square.

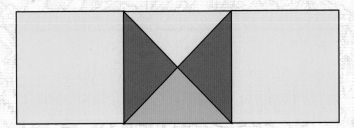

**5.** Row 2: hourglass unit, 3 ½" darkest gold square, hourglass unit.

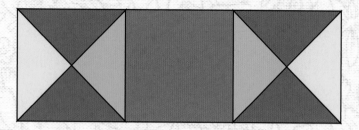

**6.** Row 3: 3 ½" light gold square, hourglass unit, 3 ½" light gold square.

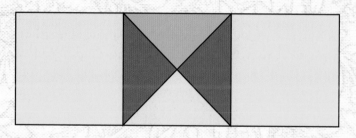

**7.** Sew the rows together as shown:

**8.** Repeat to make a total of 7 – 9 ½" blocks.

## Assembling the Quilt
**Row 1:** Star – sashing strip – star

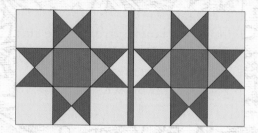

**Row 2:** Sashing strip – corner stone – sashing strip

**Row 3:** Star – sashing strip – star – sashing strip – star

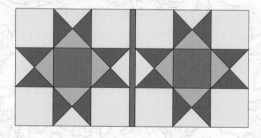

**Row 4:** Sashing strip – cornerstone – sashing strip

**Row 5:** Star – sashing strip – star

**1.** Sew row 2 to the bottom of row 1.

**2.** Sew row 3 to the bottom of row 2.
✼✼✼ *Note: the third star in row 3 is not attached to row 2, it is left unattached (see the diagram on the next page).*

**3.** Sew row 4 to the top of row 5.

**4.** Sew row 4 to the bottom of row 3.
✼✼✼*Note: the first star of row 3 is not attached to row 4.*

## Finishing
Quilt as desired. Bind.

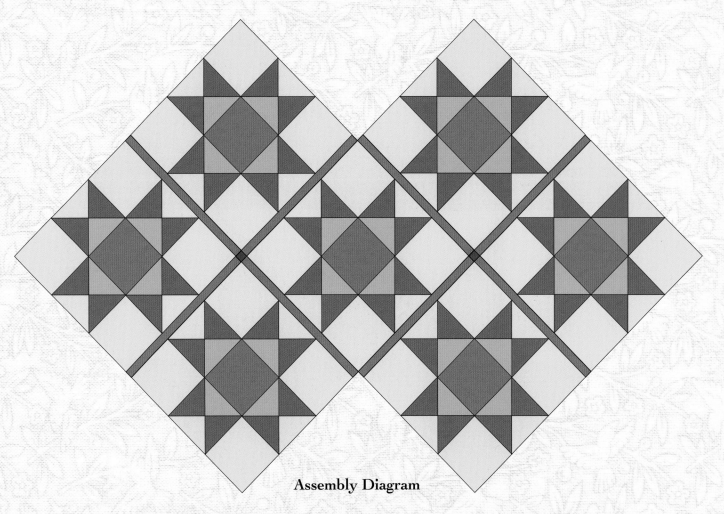

Assembly Diagram

# I'll Be Home for Christmas

## Table Topper or Tree Skirt

### 44" x 44"

Stitched by Eula Lang, embroidery by Arlene Lawson, quilted by Eula Lang

Decorating for Christmas is always fun and redwork is perfect for Christmastime. This table topper or tree skirt is a fun way to showcase your favorite of the embroidery blocks and get your house in the Christmas spirit!

## Materials Needed

- Embroidery floss (2 skeins) or 16 weight Perle cotton (1 ball) in your choice of color
- Size 7 embroidery needle
- ³/₄ yard lining or interfacing (optional) for lining the embroidery blocks
- Focus print—¹/₂ yard
- Neutral background—³/₄ yard
- Green print—1 ¹/₄ yards
- Red print—1 ¹/₄ yards

## Cutting Directions

### From the focus print:
- 1 - 13 ¹/₄" square
- 1 - 10 ³/₁₆" square, cut in half diagonally twice (4 quarter-square triangles (qst))

### From the neutral background:
- 4 - 11" squares for embroidery
- 2 - 10 ³/₁₆" squares, cut in half diagonally twice (8 qst)

### From the green print:
- 2 - 10 ³/₁₆" squares cut in half diagonally twice (8 qst)
- 18 - 4 ⁷/₈" squares cut in half diagonally once —36 half-square triangles (hst)
- 1 - 5 ¹/₄" square cut in half diagonally twice (4 qst)
- 5 - 2 ¹/₂" strips for binding (6 if you are splitting it for a tree skirt, plus a piece on the bias the length of the circumference of your circle plus 20")

### From the red print:
- 2 - 9 ⁷/₈" squares cut in half diagonally once (4 hst)
- 3 - 10 ³/₁₆" squares cut in half diagonally twice (12 qst)
- 20 - 4 ⁷/₈" squares cut in half diagonally once (40 hst)
- 1 - 5 ¹/₄" square cut in half diagonally twice (4 qst)

"I'll be home for Christmas
You can plan on me
Please have snow and mistletoe
And presents on the tree."

— I'll Be Home for Christmas

## Embroidery

Choose 4 of the embroidery motifs, trace them **on point** onto the 11" neutral squares. Line these if needed and embroider the blocks as instructed on page 12. Trim each block to 9 ¹/₂".

## Block Assembly

**1.** Sew a red 9 $7/8$" hst to each of the 4 sides of the 13 $1/4$" square of focus print. This center block will measure 18 $1/2$".

**2.** Make 4 side units by sewing 3 red, 1 focus print, 2 green and 2 neutral 10 $3/16$" qsts as shown for each side unit. These side units will measure 9 $1/2$" x 18 $1/2$".

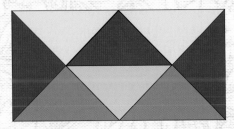

**3.** Sew 1 side unit to each side of the center square as shown.

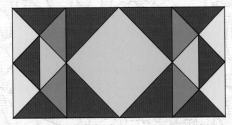

**4.** Sew an embroidered 9 $1/2$" square to each end of the remaining 2 side units as shown.

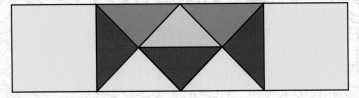

**5.** Sew the 3 units together. Your block now measures 36 $1/2$" square.

## Border

**1.** Sew 36 green 4 $7/8$" hst to 36 red 4 $7/8$" hst to make 18 hst blocks as shown.

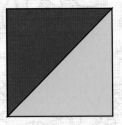

**2.** Sew 4 green 5 $1/4$" qst to 4 red 5 $1/4$" qst. Sew each of these to 1 of the remaining red 4 $7/8$" hst to make center side blocks as shown. These will measure 4 $1/2$".

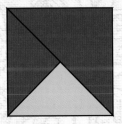

**3.** Sew 4 of the hst blocks to each side of the center side blocks as shown. Make 4 of these border strips.

**4.** Sew 1 border strip to each side of the center block with the red toward the center.

**5.** Sew the 4 remaining hst blocks to each end of the other 2 border strips.

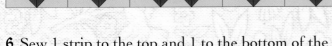

**6.** Sew 1 strip to the top and 1 to the bottom of the center block with the red toward the center. The tree skirt now measures 44 ½" square.

## Finishing

**1.** Layer backing, batting and the quilt top and quilt as desired.

**2.** Sew the 2 ½" strips together to form your binding and bind.

**Optional:** to make a tree skirt with the center hole, cut a circle out of the center to your desired size. The size will depend on whether you are using an artificial or real tree. You may audition sizes by placing bowls, cups etc or using a compass to arrive at the right size. Cut out this circle, then split the quilt from the center out to the center of one side. Bind the split and the outside edges first with a continuous piece of straight binding. After finishing that binding, bind the center cut out with the bias leaving a "tail" at end for a tie.

29

# O Tannenbaum

## 60" x 66"

Stitched by Christina DeArmond, quilted by Eula Lang

The Christmas tree is an integral part of our Christmas celebrations. We wanted to commemorate that in a quilt. This is a fun quilt to hang on your wall and makes a great tree for those who live in small spaces—just set the presents below. The quilt is beautiful as is but it would also be fun to embellish with beads, buttons and small ornaments. Have fun with it!

*Important note before starting your own O Tannenbaum quilt:* Cutting and sewing directions are for one block only. More than one of each block may be needed, the individual block directions will tell you how many to make and whether they will be used on the tree or in the background.

The suggested location for the block in the quilt is listed in parenthesis beside the name of the block. The row number will be given first followed by the block number from left to right. For example the star above the tree top will be listed as R1,B5 which stands for Row 1, Block 5. Feel free to rearrange the blocks to suit yourself, as Kaye did in the version of this quilt on the previous page.

### Abbreviations
qst=quarter-square triangle (a square cut in half diagonally twice)
hst=half-square triangle (a square cut in half diagonally once)
wof=width of fabric

All of these blocks except the Flying Geese in the border measure 6" finished, the Flying Geese are 3" x 6" finished. You will make 90 - 6 ½" blocks and 38 Flying Geese blocks.

## Fabric Requirements

- Background—15 gold and cream fabrics: ⅓ yard of each
- Tree—15 different green print fabrics: ⅓ yard of each (you will want other colors included in the prints)
- Accent (red)—¼ yard
- Doves (white)—¼ yard
- Brown tree trunk—8" square (will be trimmed)
- Binding—⅝ yard

"*Glory to God in the highest, and on earth peace, good will toward men.*"
Luke 2:14

## Cutting Directions

**For the squares:**
We'll start with the easiest block! It is the place to put that gorgeous fabric that needs to be shown off without being chopped up into little pieces.

- Background squares: cut 18 – 6 ½" squares (R1,B4, B6; R2,B2,B4,B7; R3,B1,B3,B9; R4,B7,B9; R5,B2; R6,B8; R7,B1,B9; R10,B2,B4,B6,B8)
- Tree squares: cut 4 – 6 ½" squares (R5,B5; R7,B5; R9,B2,B5)
- Tree trunk: cut 1 brown -6 ½" square (R10,B5)

# Northern Star Block

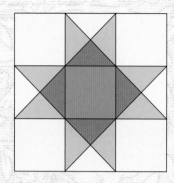

Background blocks – make 3 (R1,B1; R2,B6; R6,B2)

## Background fabric
- Cut 4 – 2 ½" square
- Cut 1 – 3 ¼" square, cut in half diagonally twice to make 4 qst

## Star points
- Cut 2 – 3 ¼" squares, cut in half diagonally twice to make 8 qst

## Accent triangles
- Cut 1 – 3 ¼" square, cut in half diagonally twice to make 8 qst

## Star center
- Cut 1 – 2 ½" square

## Cutting and Piecing the Blocks
*Note: Refer to the quilt photo on page 30 for correct color placement.*

**1.** Sew a star point qst to a background qst along the short sides, this is unit 1. Make 4.

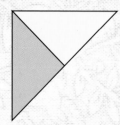

**2.** Sew a star point qst to an accent qst along short sides: this is unit 2. Make 4.

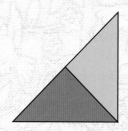

**3.** Sew unit 1 to unit 2 to make unit 3. Make 4.

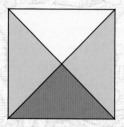

**4.** Sew the blocks into rows.
- Row 1 – 2 ½" background square, unit 3, 2 ½" background square
- Row 2 – unit 3, star center square, unit 3
- Row 3 – 2 ½" background square, unit 3, 2 ½" background square

# Windmill Block

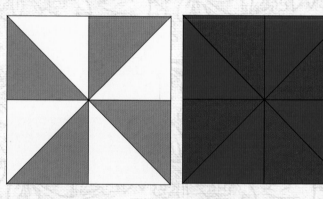

Background blocks – make 2 (R1,B2; R10,B7)
Tree blocks – make 4 (R5,B6; R7,B6; R8,B5; R9,B3)

## Cutting Instructions
- Light fabric: cut 2 – 3 ⅞" squares cut in half diagonally to make 4 hst
- Dark fabric: cut 2 – 3 ⅞" squares cut in half diagonally to make 4 hst

## Sewing Instructions
**1.** Sew 1 light hst to 1 dark hst along the long side to make a hst unit.

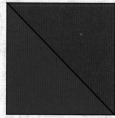

**2.** Repeat to make 4 units for each block.
**3.** Arrange the units as shown in the block and sew together.

## Four Patch Block

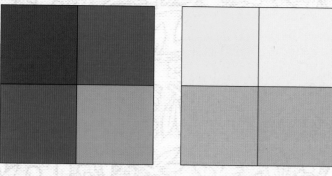

Background blocks – make 7 (R1,B3; R3,B7; R4,B1; R6, B1;B9; R10,B1,B9)
Tree blocks – make 2 (R8,B4; R9,B7)

### Cutting Instructions
Cut 4 – 3 1/2" squares for each block of a variety of fabrics

### Sewing Instructions
1. Sew 2 squares together in each of 2 rows.

2. Sew the 2 rows together.

## Dakota Star (Tree Topper) Block

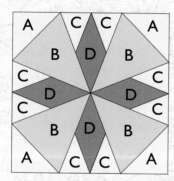

Background block – make 1 (R1,B5)

### Cutting Instructions
Use the templates on page 64.
- From the background fabric, cut 4 of template A and 8 of template C
- From the large star rays fabric, cut 4 of template B.
- From the star points fabric, cut 4 of template D.

### Sewing Instructions
Refer to the block diagram above as you sew these pieces together.
1. Sew the long side of an A triangle to the short side of a B triangle. Repeat to make 4 AB units.

2. Sew a long side of a C triangle to one side of a D diamond.

3. Sew a second C triangle to the opposite side of the D diamond. Repeat to make 4 CDC units.

4. Sew an AB unit to a CDC unit. Repeat to make 4 AB-CDC units.

5. Sew the 4 units together to make the Dakota Star block.

## Sun Ray Star Block

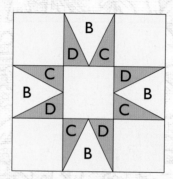

Background blocks – make 2 (R1,B7; R 5,B1)

### Cutting Instructions
Use the templates on page 64.
- From the background fabric: cut 5 – 2 1/2" squares, cut 4 of template B.
- From the star fabric: cut 4 of template C , cut 4 of template D.

### Sewing Instructions
1. Sew a C triangle to 1 side of a B triangle and a D triangle to the other side to form a DBC unit. Repeat to make 4 DBC units.

2. Piece the top and bottom rows by sewing a background square to each side of a DBC unit.

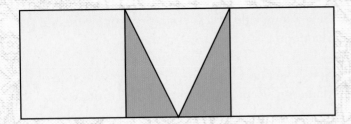

**3.** Piece the middle row by sewing 2 DBC units to each side of a background square.

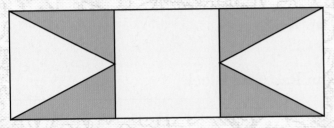

**4.** Sew the rows together.

## Double Square Block

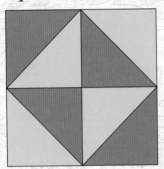

Background blocks – make 5 (R1,B8; R2,B1; R5,B9; R8,B1,B9)
Tree blocks – make 1 (R7,B4)

### Cutting Instructions
- Light fabric: cut 2 – 3 $^7/_8$" squares, cut in half diagonally once to make 4 hst.
- Dark fabric: cut 2 – 3 $^7/_8$" squares, cut in half diagonally once to make 4 hst.

### Sewing Instructions
**1.** Sew 1 light hst to 1 dark hst on the long edge to make 1 hst unit.

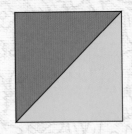

**2.** Repeat to make 4 hst units.

**3.** Arrange the units referring to the block diagrams above for placement and sew.

## Double Four Patch Block

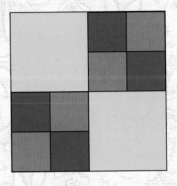

Background – make 3 (R1,B9; R3,B2; R5,B8)

### Cutting Instructions
- Medium fabric: cut 4 – 2" squares
- Light fabric: cut 2 – 3 $^1/_2$" squares
- Dark fabric: cut 4 – 2" squares

### Sewing Instructions
**1.** Make 2 small Four Patch blocks using 2 medium squares and 2 dark squares for each.

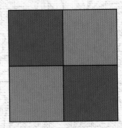

**2.** Sew a light square to 1 side of each of Four Patch referring to the block diagram for color placement. Sew these 2 together to form the Double Four Patch block.

## Turnstile Block

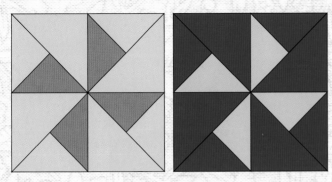

Background blocks – make 2 (R2,B3; R2,B9)
Tree blocks – make 4 (R3,B5; R5, B4; R7,B3; R8,B7)

### Cutting Instructions

Background:
- Cut 2 – 3 7/8" squares, cut in half diagonally to make 4 hst.
- Cut 1 – 4 1/4" square, cut in half twice diagonally to make 4 qst.

Fabric for star:
- Cut 1 – 4 1/4" square, cut in half twice diagonally to make 4 qst.

### Sewing Instructions

**1.** Sew 1 background qst to 1 star fabric qst along 1 short side. Repeat to make a total of 4 qst half units.

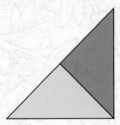

**2.** Sew a background hst to the long edge of the qst half unit. Repeat to make 4.

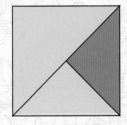

**3.** Arrange the units referring to the block diagrams above for placement and sew.

## Diamond Star Block

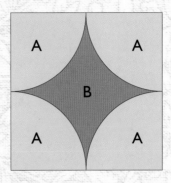

Background blocks – make 2 (R3,B8; R4,B3)
Tree blocks – make 2 (R7,B7; R9,B6)
Half background/half tree block for top of tree – make 1 (R2,B5)

### Cutting Instructions

Use templates on page 63.

- Cut 4 template A.
- Cut 1 template B.

### Sewing Instructions

**1.** Find the middle of the convex curve of an A piece by folding it in half and pin it to the center of the concave curve on 1 side of piece B.

**2.** Slowly sew the curve, stopping every few stitches to adjust the fabric. Lift the presser foot to ease in the curve.

**3.** Repeat steps 1 and 2 for the remaining sides.

*Tip:* *Sewing curved blocks will be smoother if you only use a pin on each end and one in the center.*

35

## Appliqué Blocks

Background blocks – make 2 (R2,B8; R4,B2)
(large dove)
Tree blocks – make 3 (R4,B5; R6,B4; R8,B6)
(small dove)

### Cutting Instructions
Use the templates on pages 60-61.

- Cut 1 - 7" background square.

### Sewing Instructions
1. Trace the appliqué pieces on fusible web. Reverse the direction of the dove for 1 of the background blocks and 1 of the tree blocks.

2. Roughly cut out the shapes, leaving space around each.

3. Press the fusible web onto the back of the appliqué fabric.

4. Cut the pieces out exactly on the lines.

5. Arrange the pieces onto the background square and press.

6. Hand blanket stitch or machine stitch the edges.

7. Trim the block to 6 ½".

## Drunkard's Path Block

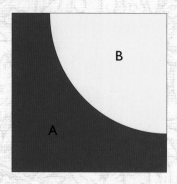

Background/tree blocks- Make 14 (R3,B4,B6; R4,B4,B6; R5,B3,B7; R6,B3,B7; R7,B2,B8; R8,B2,B8; R9,B1,B9)

### Cutting Instructions
Use templates on page 62.

- From assorted green fabrics, cut 14 template A.
- From assorted background fabrics, cut 14 template B.

### Sewing Instructions
1. Find center of each curve by folding each shape in half and marking the center with a pin.

2. Match the center of piece A to the center of piece B and pin.

3. Slowly sew the pieces together stopping every few stitches to line up the fabric (you may need to lift the presser foot to adjust the fabric). Repeat to make 14 blocks.

## Birds in Flight Block

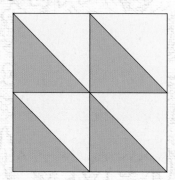

Background blocks- make 2 (R4,B8; R10,B3)

### Cutting Instructions
- Light fabric: cut 2 – 3 ⅞" squares, cut in half

diagonally once to make 4 hst
  • From dark fabric: cut 2 – 3 ⁷/₈" squares, cut in half diagonally once to make 4 hst

## Sewing Instructions
**1.** Sew the long edges of 1 light hst to 1 dark hst. Make 4.

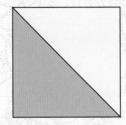

**2.** Refer to the block above for color placement and sew the 4 squares together.

## Snowball Blocks

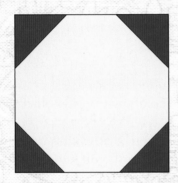

Tree blocks – make 3 (R6,B5; R8,B3; R9,B8)

## Cutting Instructions
  • Large print fabric: cut 1 – 6 ½" square
  • Green fabric: cut 4 – 2 ½" squares

## Sewing Instructions
**1.** Draw a diagonal line from corner to corner on the back of the 4 tree squares.

**2.** Place a green square in each corner of the 6 ½" square.

**3.** Sew on the diagonal line.

**4.** Trim off the outer triangle ¼" past the stitched line.

**5.** Press the triangle open.

## Crosses of Christmas Block

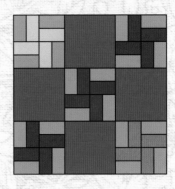

Tree blocks – make 2 (R6,B6; R9,B4)

## Cutting Instructions
  • Crosses: use 5 different fabrics, from *each* of them cut 4 – 1" x 1 ½" rectangles
  • Tree fabric: 20 – 1" x 1 ½" rectangles
  • Second tree print: cut 4 – 2 ½" squares

## Sewing Instructions
**1.** Sew 1 - 1" x 1 ½" rectangle of tree fabric to one 1" x 1 ½" rectangle accent fabric along the long side to make a 1 ½" square. Repeat with the other 3 sets of rectangles.

**2.** Sew 2 1 ½" squares together turning the second one as shown. Repeat with the other 2 squares.

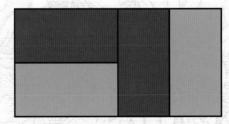

**3.** Sew these 2 units together to form the 2 ½" square cross.

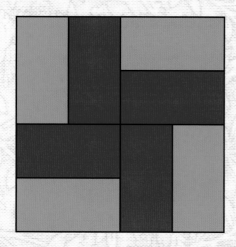

**4.** Repeat to make 1 cross with each of the 4 other fabrics.

**5.** For rows 1 and 3 sew 1 cross unit to each side of the second tree print square.

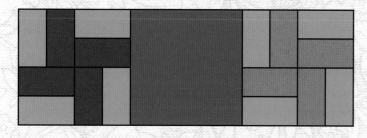

**6.** For row 2 sew 1 tree print square to each side of a cross unit.

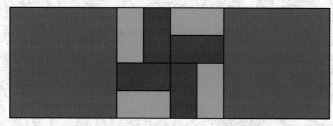

**7.** Sew the 3 rows together to form your block.

## Assembling the Quilt

Sew the blocks together into the rows as listed under each block. You can also arrange blocks within the tree or the background as desired, keeping the Drunkards' Path blocks in the same place to form the outer edge of the tree.

## Flying Geese Border

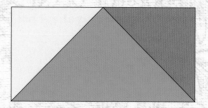

Make 38 flying geese.

### Cutting Instructions

Assorted tree fabrics:
- Cut 10 – 7 ¼" squares, cut in half diagonally twice (40 qst—only 38 will be used).
- Cut 2 - 3 ⅞" squares, cut in half diagonally once (4 hst).

Assorted background fabrics:
- Cut 40 – 3 ⅞" squares, cut in half diagonally once (80 hst).

### Sewing Instructions

*Note: these instructions are for 1 flying geese block (you need 38 of these blocks).*

**1.** Sew a background hst to *each* short side of a tree qst, mixing the colors within the blocks.

**2.** Sew a tree hst to a background hst to make a corner square. Repeat until you have 4 corner squares.

**3.** Sew 2 strips of 10 flying geese blocks.

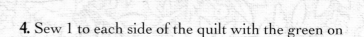

**4.** Sew 1 to each side of the quilt with the green on the outside.

**5.** Sew 2 sets of 9 flying geese blocks. Sew a corner square to each end.

**6.** Sew 1 to the top and 1 to the bottom edge of the quilt, with the green on the outside..

**7.** Quilt as desired.

**8.** Cut 7 - 2 ½" x wof strips from the binding fabric. Bind.

**9.** Decorate and enjoy your tree!

Assembly Diagram

# Embroidery Patterns

On the pages that follow are patterns for the embroidery patterns for the *Christmases Remembered* quilt, followed by *O Tannenbaum* pattern templates.

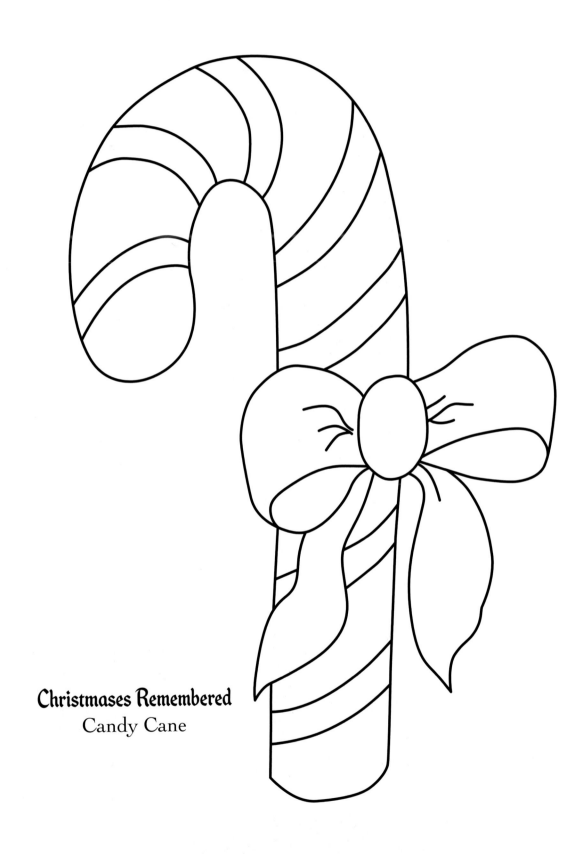

**Christmases Remembered**
Candy Cane

**Christmases Remembered**
Candles

**Christmases Remembered**
Red Bird

**Christmases Remembered**

Peace Dove

**Christmases Remembered**
Angel

**Christmases Remembered**
Snowflake

**Christmases Remembered**
Gift

**Christmases Remembered**
Holly

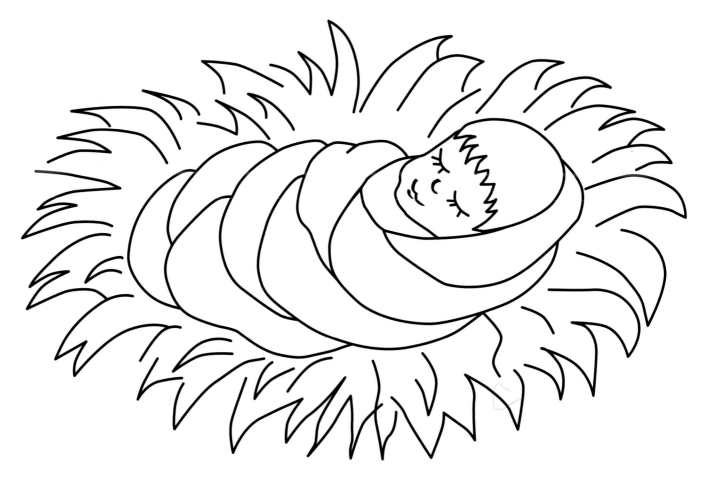

**Christmases Remembered**
Baby Jesus

**Christmases Remembered**
Bell

**Christmases Remembered**
Sled

**Christmases Remembered**
Bible

**Christmases Remembered**
Rocking Horse

**Christmases Remembered**
Poinsettia

**Christmases Remembered**
Joy

**Christmases Remembered**
Train

**Christmases Remembered**
Gingerbread Man

**Christmases Remembered**
Stocking

**Christmases Remembered**

Snowman

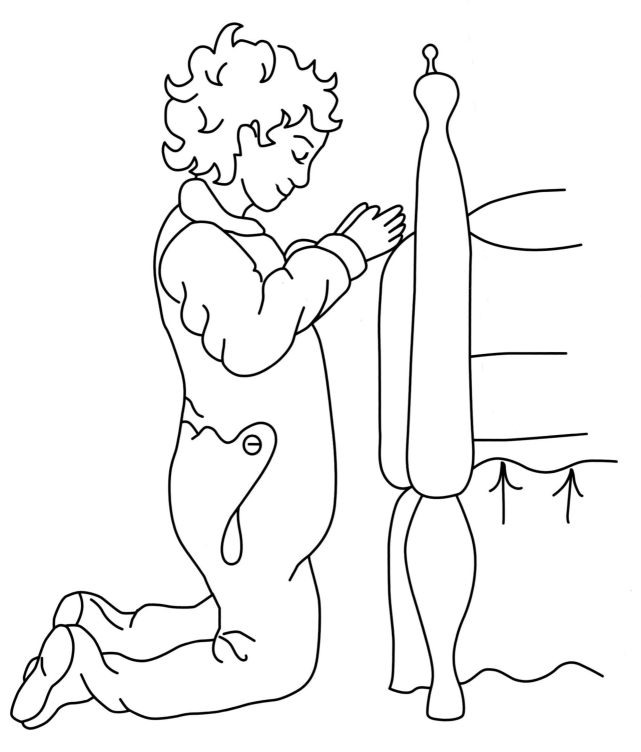

**Christmases Remembered**
Prayer Time

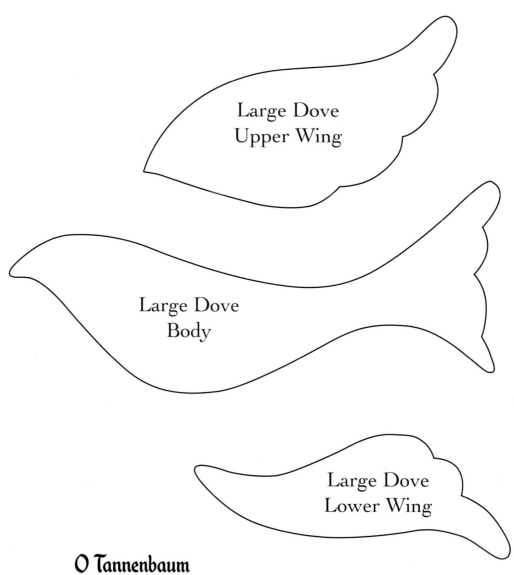

Large Dove
Upper Wing

Large Dove
Body

Large Dove
Lower Wing

## O Tannenbaum
Dove for background blocks.
Make one and one reversed.

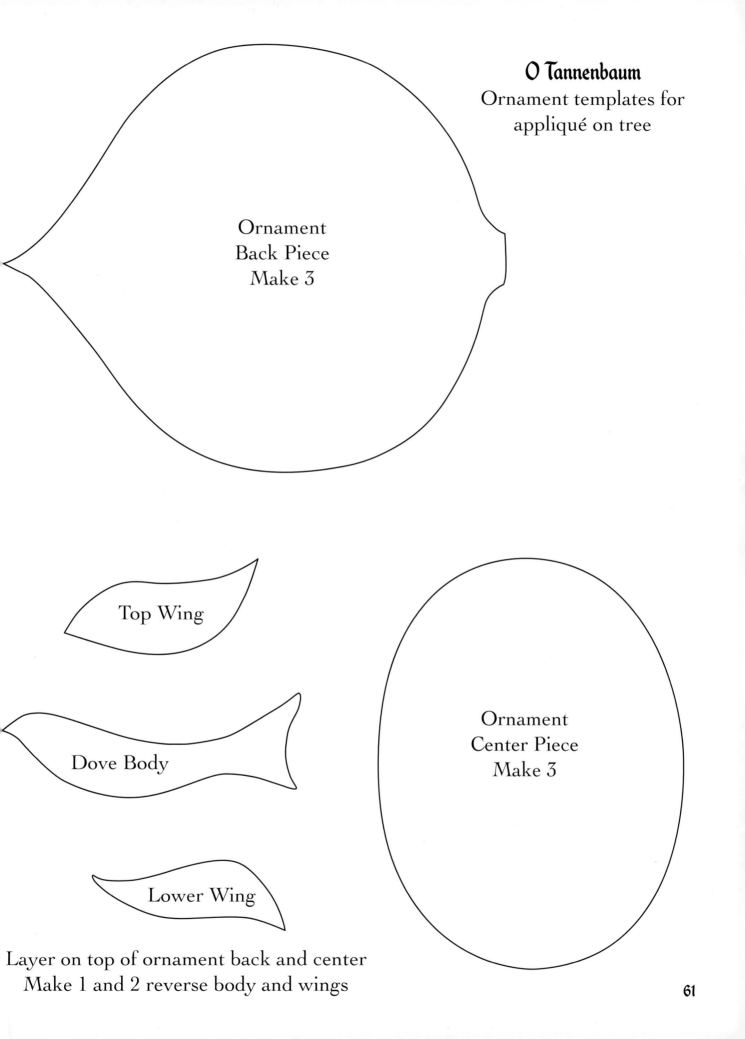

O Tannenbaum
Ornament templates for
appliqué on tree

Ornament
Back Piece
Make 3

Top Wing

Dove Body

Lower Wing

Ornament
Center Piece
Make 3

Layer on top of ornament back and center
Make 1 and 2 reverse body and wings

61

## O Tannenbaum
### Drunkard's Path Block

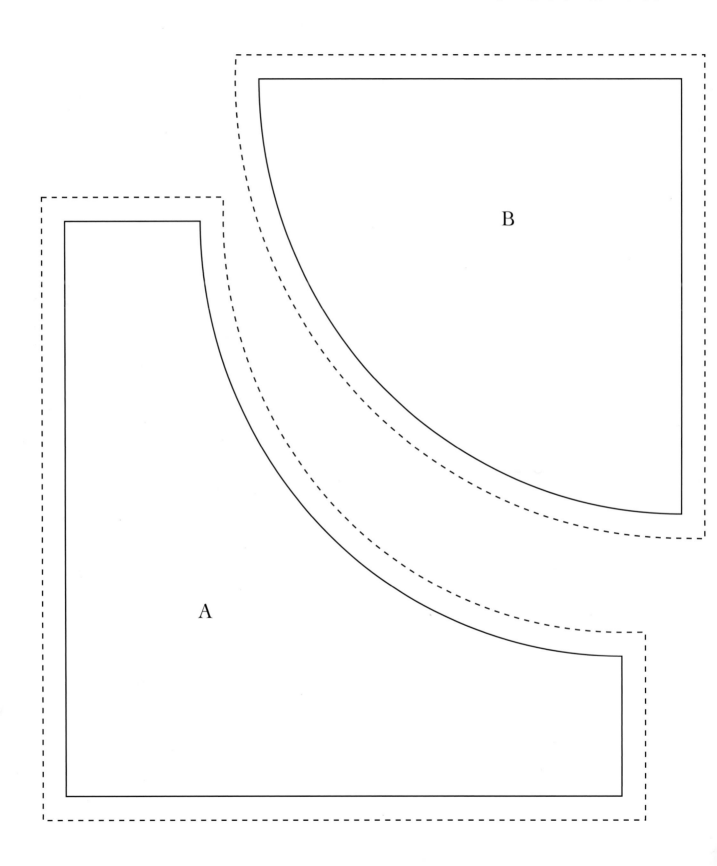

B

A

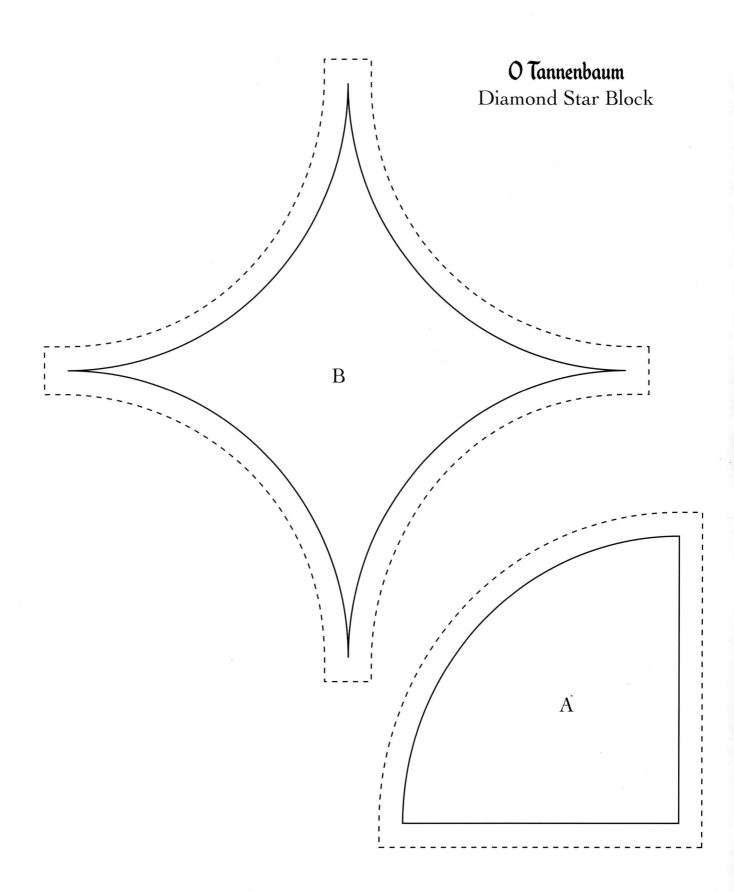

O Tannenbaum
Diamond Star Block

B

A

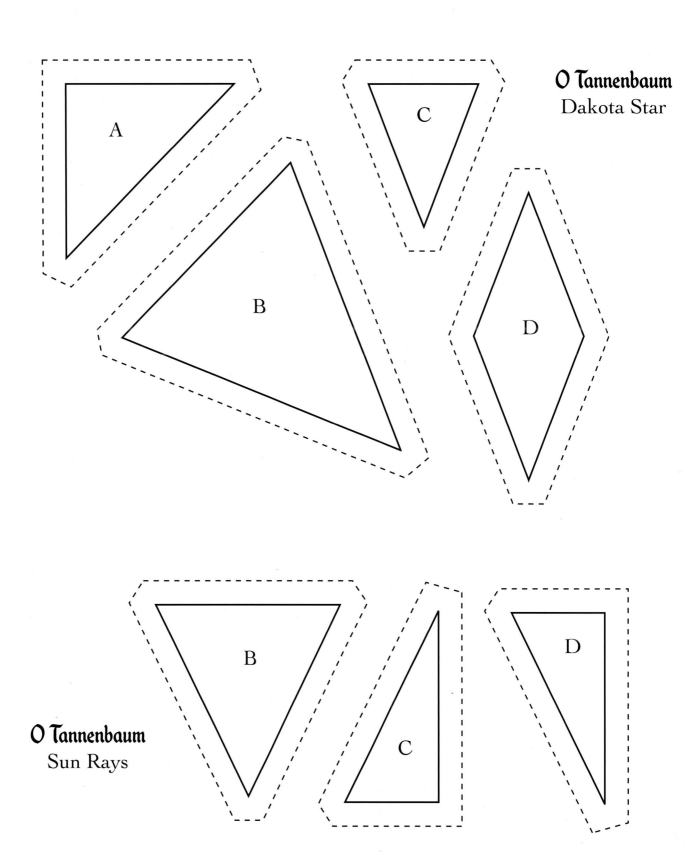

**O Tannenbaum**
Dakota Star

A

B

C

D

**O Tannenbaum**
Sun Rays

B

C

D